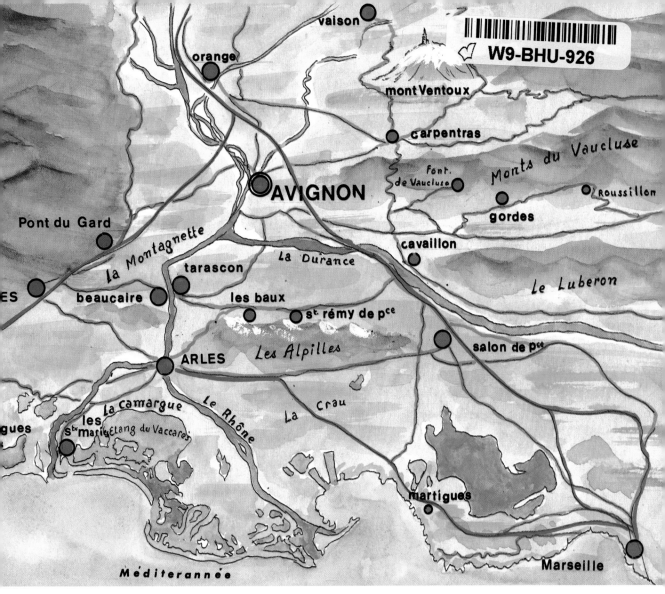

Avignon, gateway to the delta

THE ORIGINS OF AVIGNON

The location of Avignon on a giant rock, which dominates the alluvial plain from a height of more than 30 metres, where the durance flows into the Rhône, has attracted man's attention throughout the ages by its exceptional strategic nature.

In fact, recent archaeological research has shown that the Rocher des Doms has been lived on since neolothic times. At that period, the beach which extended to the south-west of the **oppidum,** on the side of the Rhône where the Place du Palais is now, was occupied by an already dense and organised population. If one can judge by its extent and richness, the settlement established to the north-west of Avignon must have been one of the largest in the Rhône valley about the end of the 3rd milennium BC, whilst the people of Crete were building the first palace of Knossos and the Pharaohs of the XII dynasty were reigning over Egypt.

Finds dating to this period, made during excavations on the Avignon site, are considerable in number: – various earthenware vases, tools and weapons of chipped flint, of polished stone, worked leather, daggers and awls of copper, limestone grinding wheels, etc. But the most important finds from this period are doubtless two Old Stone Age burials and an anthropomorphic stela dated to the Bronze age, discovered on the Rocher des Doms and which constitutes the oldest sign of art in Avignon. Many of these items are currently on show in the Musée de Préhistoire vauclusienne at the Calvet Museum.

If the Bronze or Chalcolithic Age belongs to the Prehistoric period, that which extends from the dawn of the Bronze Age to the Conquest of Gaul is called the Protohistoric Period. It is one of transition, during which the invention of bronze, then the use of iron, gave developing techniques a new impulsion which was to intensify the cultural and commercial exchanges between tribes to a degree never before realised. The Rhône was, at every period, a way of acccess and exchange. It was through the Rhône valley that the peoples of the Mediterranean brought to the so-called 'barbarians' the many products of their brilliant civilisation. Equally, it was by the Rhône that they received tin from the Scilly Isles, amber from the Artic regions, as well as many other precious and useful materials. A large part of this traffic would necessarily pass by Avignon. At first a native trading post, the settlement later came under the influence of Marseilles, without however losing its autonomy, which allowed the town, from the II century BC, to mint its own coins, though these were only imitations of those of Marseilles.

It was probably during the Protohistoric period that the ancient **Avenio** acquired its name. Of Celtic or Ligurian origin, it means, according to savants, either "River Town" or "Town of violent wind", both ideas being just as likely as not.

The famous anthropomorphic stela found on the rocher des Doms, which is the oldest art object yet found belonging to Avignon. It dates to the Bronze Age (end of the 3rd milennium BC) and shows a very stylised human head with, at bottom right, a solar sign. (musée Calvet, Galerie de préhistoire vauclusienne).

IN ANTIQUITY

After the fall of Marseilles, in 49 BC, Avignon was taken away from the control of the latter to become, it seems, the site of a Volscian territorial city. This was the time when Julius Cæsar, after his victory, organised the Narbonnaise region along sound lines and created colonies for his veterans, notably those of Avignon, Orange, Apt and Carpentras. The Avignon Colony stretched from the heights of Bédarrides-Châteauneuf in the north as far as Saint-Rémy and Eyguières in the south ; in the east, it went from the Rhône to the hills of Vedène and Caumont.

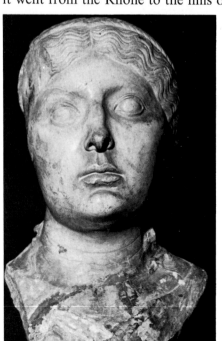

Lapidary Museum

◄ *Head attributed to Julia Drusilla (1st century) found near the Cathedral of N.D. des Doms*

Head of a statue attributed to Drusus the Younger (white marble from the 1st century) found in the course of excavations, Place de l'Horloge. ►

Avignon became one of the 80 cities of Gaul in the days of Emperor Augustus, then received the title of Latin colony under Claudius. It was however only in the II century AD, under Hadrian, that Avignon achieved the grade of Roman City, just 70 years before the edict of Caracalla which extended that privilege to all cities in Gaul.

Without equalling the size of Arles or Nîmes, gallo-roman Avignon made up an agglomeration the size of which may be estimated at 46 hectares, according to the area over which remains have been found and what one knows of the lines of its defences. Joseph Girard estimated that population was about 27 000 inhabitants, at least during the prosperous period of the I and II centuries AD.

How then to explain that there remains almost no visible trace of this opulent past? To admit this surprising fact, it should not be forgotten that in the XIV century, Avignon became the capital of the Christian world, and one of the most populated cities in the west. To build the immense pontifical palace and the innumerable quarters, convents, houses, etc., to shelter this multitude, the builders did not hesitate to transform old monuments into stone quarries. The succeeding centuries completed this destruction, wiping out bit by bit the last traces of that which had been gallo-roman Avignon.

It still happens, in the course of roadworks, that the Avignon soil reveals some of the secrets of its gallo-roman past which were effaced during the Middle Ages. Recent large-scale excavations have confirmed the fact that the Roman forum was situated on the site of the present Hôtel de Ville and the Municipal Theatre. One can see, to the west of the Mairie, on the edge of the Rue Racine, a few large remnants of buildings which formed part of this monumental group. A few architectural and sculptural fragments are to be seen in the **Musée Lapidaire** (annexe to the Calvet Museum, Rue de la République).

Partial view of the Gallo-Roman remains found in the Rue Racine. These foundations, which belonged to a large monument in the Forum, continue under the Town Hall.

Head of Jupiter Serapis found at Avignon (white marble, 1st century). Only the head is antique, the bust being a modern reconstruction (Musée Lapidaire).

3

THE MIDDLE AGES

After the barbarian invasions which marked the fall of the Roman Empire, Avignon shrank around the original **oppidum,** the Rocher des Doms, within a reduced perimeter which encompassed only a seventh of the former area (according to J. Girard). Nevertheless, the town did not in any way lose its strategic importance. An advanced citadel of the Burgundian kingdom, heavily fortified, Avignon was besieged in vain by Clovis in 500 AD, and was thenceforth under the tenure of Bourgogne.

The Rocher des Doms in the XVII century (drawing aft 1650, date of an explosion in the Fort Saint-Martin).

During the first half of the VIII century the Arabs, already established in the ancient province of Septimania across the Rhône, invaded Provence and made of Avignon one of their surest stongholds. It took Charles Martel no less than two sieges (in 737 and 739) to dislodge them.

Next, Avignon was linked in succession with the Empire of Charlemagne, the Kingdom of Aquitaine, the kingdom of Lothair, the kingdom of Provence and finally, in the XI century with the Germanic Holy roman Empire.

At the beginning of the XII century, Provence was shared between three houses : Toulouse, Urgel and Barcelona. The rivalry between these three families provoked a war (siege of Orange in 1123) and various share-outs, but Avignon always remained undivided, the three sides having agreed on the creation of a neutral zone at the point where the three counties met.

The feudal system was the cause of the dilution of power and the fragmentation of the territory, thus provoking the coming of the Communes. "At Avignon the new system, often called by the convenient but inexact name of Republic, was established in 1129." (J. Girard). The city found itself henceforth freed from the authority of the counts and the viscount and, for more than a half century, had at its head elected magistrates called consuls or podestas who, under the presidence of the bishop, effectively exercised power. As a collective authority, the city of Avignon had only the duties of a vassal towards his suzerain as far as the counts were concerned.

This new system brought new prosperity to Avignon which became a cosmopolitan city of trade and passage. The end of the XII century saw the construction of the pont St.Bénézet over the Rhône. The Cathedral (Notre-Dame-des-Doms) and the St.Ruf Abbey were enlarged afresh, and a new ring of ramparts were built, much bigger than the old one of the early Middle Ages.

At the beginning of the XIII century, during the Albigensian Crusade, Avignon took the side of the Count of Toulouse. Contingents from the Commune contributed to the victory of the Toulousains before Beaucaire in 1216. In 1218, men from Avignon beat the Prince of Orange; Guillaume des Baux, the usurper of the Comtat Venaissin took him prisoner and cut his throat. The Avignon Commune "then reached the peak of its power and felt strong enough to face up to the king of France and the Church." But in 1226, Louis VIII, accompanied by the Papal Legate and a powerful army, marched down the Rhône Valley. This immense army arrived at the gates of Avignon on the 10th June. Then began a memorable siege which became one of the great military events of the Middle Ages. On 12th September, 1226, after three months resistance, the people of Avignon had to capitulate, beaten by hunger. The ramparts were demolished, as well as 300 fortified houses. Finally Louis VIII had the greater part of the Pont St.Bénézet dismantled.

Hastened by the death of Frederick II, the break-up of the imperial party led finally to the abolition of the Commune of Avignon, sanctioned by the Convention of Beaucaire the 7th May, 1251.

In 1274 the Holy See took possession of the Comtat Venaissin and, in 1290, Charles II of Anjou, Count of Provence, became the sole master of Avignon.

Nothing remains from the early Middle Ages at Avignon; from the later part we have Notre-Dame-des-Doms, (much remade), the old Palais de la Commune, (much altered), the Pont St.Bénézet (especially the lower chapel), and the remains of the St.Ruf Abbey. A few inscriptions from the XI and XII centuries, as well as a fine series of Romanesque capitals are to be found in the Petit-Palais Museum.

View of the ruins of the abbey of St.Ruf-hors-les-murs, built at the end of the XII century on the site of an early Christian basilica.

The St.Ruf Abbey was built at the end of the XII century, on the site of a suburban hermitage from the X century, which had itself succeeded an early christian place of worship dating back to the IV century. Nothing remains of the monastic buildings nor of the magnificent cloister built with the largesse of Pope Adrian IV. On the contrary, despite much damage and the demolition of the entire nave in 1763, the remains of the abbey church, still impressive, offer one of the best examples of Romanesque architecture in the region. They comprise just the apse, its chapels and the transept, flanked on the south-west by a square bell-tower. Situated in the countryside, the church must have been fortified in the XIV century, and it is from this period which date the battlements which still crown the transept.

Excavations made in 1975, on the site of the vanished nave, revealed the existence of an early Christian cemetery. The oldest sarcophagii yet brought to light may be dated to the V and VI centuries AD.

Despite their distance from the centre of town, the remains of the Abbey Church of St.Ruf, as well as the old necropolis, are worth the small detour.

General view of the west side of the Palais des Papes. At right, the "Palais neuf" of Clement VI. In the centre, the "Palais vieux" of Benedict XII. At left, the belfry and porch of the Cathedral N.D. des Doms.

THE XIV CENTURY: THE AVIGNON POPES

The XIV century opened well for Avignon, which was to experience for almost 200 years an era of prosperity without precedent in the annals of national history. in fact, the installation of the papacy within its walls from 1309, rapidly made this small feudal city into the capital of Christendom, and one of the most flourishing towns of the known world.

At this time bursting with five to six thousand inhabitants, squeezed within decaying walls, nothing suggested this town would have such a great destiny.

Yet the reasons which led the Sovereign Pontiffs to choose Avignon were not the fruit of sheer chance; they are well known and based on politics and geography. On the one hand, the town belonged to Charles of Anjou, Count of Provence, and faithful vassal of the Church as King of Naples. On the other, the Comtat Venaissin, an adjoining territory, had been Papal proprety since 1274. In addition, at the beginning of the XIV century, the country was steeped in peace, which was certainly not the case in Rome, then being torn apart by rival factions. Finally, placed at the junction of the Rhône and the Durance, both lines of communication, the site of Avignon seemed particularly favorable for international relations.

Clement V, the first of the Avignon Popes, was a wandering Pope. Elected at Perugia in 1305 and crowned at Lyons, he only arrived at Avignon in 1309, and set up his court in the vast Dominican convent.

John XXII, who succeeded him in 1316, did not experience this unstable situation, since he had been Bishop of Avignon. As soon as he was elected he moved the Papal residence to his old episcopal palace, and turned it into a "fortified house".

On the Palais des Papes square

It was only under Benedict XII (1334-1342) that Avignon became the normal place of residence of the pontiffs, and that construction of the Palais des Papes began.

His successor, Clement VI, a fine pope and patron of the arts, enlarged the apostolic acquaintance and attracted to his court numerous artists from Italy and the North, especially painters, a meeting which was at the origin of the fusion which gave birth to the Avignon school. In addition, in 1348, he bought the town from the famous Queen Jeanne of Naples, Countess of Provence.

Innocent VI (1352-1362) completed the construction of the palace, and also undertook to build new defences, on other words the famous ramparts which are today one of the attractions of the city.

As for Urban V (1362-1370), he was preoccupied with the project of his return to Rome, which he realised in 1367, but this was only termporary, for the Pope found he could not live there; the city being in the grip of agitators, any kind of government was impossible. He therefore returned to Avignon in 1370, to die there.

Gregory XI, elected the same year, realised his predecessor's dream of reestablishing the Holy See on the banks of the Tiber in 1376. His death at Rome in 1378 put an end to the dinasty of French Popes.

Shortly afterwards an Italian was proclaimed Pope, with the name of Urban VI, but his roughness towards the cardinals and his awkwardness pushed these latter, withdrawn to Agnani, to declare the election nul and void, obtained under duress, and to choose another pope. From Savoy, Robert de Geneva was elected at Fondi, and came to reside at Avignon. Thus began the great Schism in the West which divided Christianity into two obediences, and at the same time took away from Avignon its title of Capital of Christendom.

At the death of Clement VII in 1394, it was Pedro de Luna, from Aragon, who was proclaimed, and who took the name of Benedict XIII. However, on seeing that the Holy See did not obey him, this obstinate old man locked himself in the Palais des Papes with his followers, where he was blockaded by the townspeople and dissenting cardinals. After his eventual departure, his nephew Rodrigue de Luna continued to resist in the fortress, and did not yield until 1411. Since then Avignon has seen no more of the Vicar of Christ.

These imposing walls were worthy of the pomp of the Papacy. If the interior was totally stripped of its riches and treasures, the palace which served then as jewel-case reminds us of the power of the Church in the Middle Ages.

This long period of presence of the papacy had completely changed the face of the town. It had become a large agglomeration, grouping in the course of the century nearly 30 000 souls despite the hecatomb produced by the Plagues of 1348 and 1361. The Pontifical court had conferred on the town an unequalled prosperity in every direction, and numerous monuments remain witness to this glorious period. The most spectacular is doubtless the Palais des Papes, but one should also mention a number of places of worship built in the same century to replace earlier buildings in disrepair or which had become too small. Such is the case of the St.Agricol, St.Pierre and St.Didier churches, which all offer interesting elements of architecture or of Gothic sculpture, the latter being also represented by an important series of funerary monuments.

One should also note the cardinals' houses, or "livrées", including that of Ceccano, recently restored, which give an idea of the importance of these princely palaces, most of which, unfortunately, have been disfigured or destroyed.

An even more ruthless end was in store for the houses of the bourgeois, which have all been demolished in the course of the centuries, to the extent that it is no longer possible to see a single building of this type in a town which still had hundreds standing in the XV century.

Fortunately, the Palais des Papes is still there, dominating the city with its high walls and reminding the passer-by of the days of magnificence of a by-gone century, gone for ever.

Night view of the Porte des Champeaux, main entrance of the Palais ▶

Aerial view of the Palais des Papes, the Petit Palais, the Pont St.Bénézet and Villeneuve-lès-Avignon.

AVIGNON IN THE DAYS OF THE LEGATES (XV to XVI c.)

Following the departure of the papacy, Avignon was governed for almost two centuries by legates named by the Pope. The most eminent amongst them were the Cardinal Pierre de Foix (1433-1464), Julien de la Rovère (1476-1503), who later became Pope Julius II, Alexandre Farnese (1541-1565), and the Cardinal Georges d'Armagnac (1565-1585). Under the rule of these Princes of the Church and despite numérous difficulties created by the Kings of France, in particular Louis IX and François I, the town tried to keep some part of the riches and prestige which it had acquired in the XIV century. The Church almost completely succeeded in keeping Avignon out of the Wars of Religion.

Weaving, tanning, silk production and papermaking developed considerably, whilst business maintained a good level. "Avignon was no longer the centre of the Christian world, but governed by high-born Legates with extended powers, it remained an important political centre, a place of freedom and asylum, a neutral island in the midst of troubled provinces" (J. Sautel *et al*, 1944).

Despite a net decline in its University, Avignon remained a large cultural centre and, thanks to its artists, especially its School of painting, one of the largest art centres of the XV century.

At the centre of the Wars of Religion, under the impetus of Cardinal d'Armagnac and Archbishop Taurusi, Avignon became one of the principal fiefs of the Counter-Reform.

The days of the Legates have left Avignon with numerous architectural souvenirs, notably the Celestins church, the frontage of St.Pierre and of Petit-Palais, the Baroncelli mansion (or Palais du Roure), the peal of bells of the Hôtel de Ville, etc. Sculpture is principally represented by the famous "transi" of Cardinal Lagrange (Petit-Palais), the Bearing of the Cross by Francesco Laurana (St.Didier church) and the reredos of the Doni, by Imbert Boachon (St.Agricol church). In painting, the famous "Avignon School", which is in reality only a grouping of artists of diverse origins and diverse tendencies, was above all illustrated by Bertrand de la Barre, Enguerrand Quarton (author of the famous "Crowning of the Virgin" at Villeneuve-lès-Avignon), Nicolas Froment, Pierre Villate and Simon de Châlons. Part of these works may be seen at the Petit-Palais Museum.

The Popes' Palace at the end of the XVII century (Calvet Museum)

THE PERIOD OF VICE-LEGATES (XVII-XVIII c.)

'Happy peoples have no history': this saying may be applied to Avignon of the XVII and XVIII centuries, if one forgets the quarrel of the "Pevoulins and the Pessugaux", where popular elements and the nobility clashed, as well as numerous meddlings by the French monarchy which culminated in three temporary occupations (1662-64, 1688-89, and 1768-74). This apart, and despite an administration often pusillanimous and retrograde by vice-Legates who exercised authority on behalf of Legates far away in Rome, Avignon and the Pontifical states remained outside the troubles which upset the neighbouring provinces.

"Despite favourable conditions, economic life was slowed by the inertia of local powers and the protectionist barrieres which closed off the kingdom. All improvements arose from private initiative... The paper trade, printing, painted or dyed cotton goods, these counted amongst the most prosperous industries; but the most important was that of silk" (J. Sautel *et al,* 1944). Avignon's situation, enclosed within another kingdom, encouraged a huge contraband trade (tobacco, printed cottons, publications, playing cards, etc.), which was to be vigorously fought by the French administration (Concordat of 1734).

During the time of the vice-Legates, the relative peace which Avignon enjoyed and its cosmopolitanism encouraged a vigorous growth of culture and the arts. The teaching of the Jesuits, litterary life, music, the theatre, all developed rapidly. Painting is illustrated by artists such as Guillaume Grève, Nicolas and Pierre Mignard, the Parrocels, Philippe Sauvan and Joseph Vernet, whilst the Péru dynasty almost completely monopolised the sculpture scene. But it is above all the architectural legacy of which we may be proud: chapels, family mansions, town houses or official buildings. Amongst the best known may be mentioned architects François de Royers de la Valfenière, Jean-André Borde, Pierre Mignard, the Franque and Péru dynasties (the latter both sculptors and architects), Thomas Lainé, Jean-Ange Brun, Abel Mottard, etc. The architectural style, inspired by Italy in the first half of the XVII century, next underwent the influence of French classicism. Among the most noteworthy monuments of this period may be mentioned the chapel of the Jesuit college, (now the Musée Lapidaire, Rue de la République), and that of La Visitation, (Rue Paul-Saïn), The Mint, (facing the Palais), the mansion of the Ducs de Crillon (Rue du Roi-René), and that of the Galléans des Issarts (Rue du Four), the St.Marthe Hospital and the Saint Charles Seminary, the de Caumont house (Boulevard Raspail), and that of de Villeneuve-Martignan (at present the Calvet Museum, Rue Joseph-Vernet), the Black Penitents' Chapel (Rue Banasterie), and that of the Oratory (Rue Joseph-Vernet), the Salt warehouse (Rue Remparts-St-Lazare), the old Comedy theatre (Place Crillon), etc.

Plan of the Pope's Palace

① *The Porte des Champeaux, entrance to the court of Honour.* ② *The Tour de la Campane.* ③ *The Tour de Trouillas.* ④ *The Tour de la Glacière; the Tour des Cuisines (chimney).* ⑤ *Wing of the Familiars; the Cloister Benedict XII; the Conclave wing.* ⑥ *The Tour de la Gache; the Cour d'Honneur.* ⑦ *The Hall of the Consistory.* ⑧ *The Chapel of St.John; the Chapel of St.Martial.* ⑨ *The Tour du Pape, or Des Anges.* ⑩ *The Tour St.Laurent.* ⑪ *The Tour de la Garde-robe.* ⑫ *The Hall of the Great Audience; the Great Chapel.* ⑬ *The corner tower.* ⑭ *The Cathedral of Notre-Dame des Doms.*

Only two Popes were directly concerned with the building of the Palais des Papes at Avignon: Benedict XII who, between 1335 and 1342, raised the buildings which we call **Le Palais-Vieux,** and Clement VI, who built the southern part, known as **Le Palais-Neuf.**

From the beginning of his pontificate Benedict XII found the old Bishop's Palace, used by his predecessor John XXII, too small. He bought the building, demolished it, and built on its site the northern part of the present Palais des Papes. His architect was Pierre Poisson, from the Ariège region.

Clement VI, who succeeded him bought the houses to the south of the Palais-Vieux, razed them to the ground, and constructed on this space the two large wings which together constitute the Palais-Neuf, – the Audience wing to the south, and that of the Dignitaries to the west. He had for architect a man from the Île-de-France, Jean de Louvres, but for the frescoes he called in an Italian, Matteo Gioivannetti, a native of Viterbo. Innocent VI (1352-1362), completed the work by the construction of two towers, that of St.Laurent and the Tour de la Gâche.

Whilst the palace of Benedict XII calls attention by its great austerity, which corresponded to the tastes of this Pope, who was a former Cistercian monk, that of Clement VI, of a much more evolved architecture, appears to us as the mirror of this pontiff, who was a great Lord and patron of the arts.

The present-day visitor to the monument is able to visit the greater part of these two palaces.

Entrance is made by the **Porte des Champeaux,** which is the main entrance to the palace of Clement VI. From there one enters the **Cour d'Honneur,** formed by the junction of the two palaces. Here is the powerful **Tour des Anges** or **Tour du Pape,** which held the pontifical treasure, and where the Pope had his bedroom. Next, passing the Conclave wing, entrance is made into the old Palace by a fortified passage leading to the cloister of Benedict XII, of which the forecourt constitutes the centre of Benedict's buildings. From the Lower gallery can be seen the large chapel built by Benedict, the **Tour de la Campane,** and the wing of the Familiars, which is topped to the south by the belfry of the **Cloche d'Argent.**

The Porte des Champeaux: the turrets and the armorial bearings of Clement VI, above the entrance. At right, the watch-turret and, in the background, the Tour de la Campane.

The Court of Honour which joined the old and new palaces, point of departure of the guided tour. This view was taken from the Conclave Room.

Next we enter the **Consistory,** a large room 34 metres long where the cardinals met together under the presidence of the Pope. The paintings which decorated the walls were destroyed by a fire in 1413. On the eastern side is the opening into the **Chapelle Saint-Jean,** which contains admirable frescoes attributed to Matteo Giovanetti showing the principal episodes in the life of two saints, John the Baptist and John the Evangelist. On the west wall are hung the precious frescoes and synoptics by Simone Martini, from the gateway of Notre-Dame-des-Doms.

Two views of the Consistory. On the walls are exhibited frescoes and sinopies of Simone Martini, coming from the porch of N.D. des Doms, as well as portraits of the Avignon Popes.

The Consistory

At the end of the Consistory, XIX century portraits of the Avignon Popes

The St.John chapel

West wall: the Crucifixion: Christ confides the Virgin to St.John.

East wall of the palace, the left-hand tower holds the St.John chapel on a level with the Consistory, above, the St.Martial chapel is level with the Grand Tinel (refectory), the kitchen of which, at right, is surmounted by an octogonal chimney. ▼

THE GRAND TINEL

The Grand Tinel, or banqueting hall

By the stairs runing along the north gallery of the cloister, one reaches the upper gallery which gives access to the **Grand Tinel,** a vast room of 48 metres long, roofed by a panelled vault, (restored). This was the banqueting hall. On the east side, a door gives on to the **Chapelle de Saint-Martial,** built directly above that of Saint-Jean.

This charming oratory also contains a r markable group of frescoes painted by Matt Giovannetti and represents, in detail, the "l gend" of St.Martial, apostle of Limousin. To t north of the Grand Tinel, one may see the **Cuisi Haute,** constructed by Clement VI and conta ning a large pyramidal chimney, one of t curiosities of the Palais des Papes.

Gobelin Tapestries, on show in the Grand Tinel (State loan)

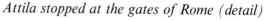

The victory of Constantine (detail)

Attila stopped at the gates of Rome (detail)

THE ST.MARTIAL CHAPEL

St.Martial Chapel. painted ceiling: scenes from the life of St.Martial: Childhood, youth, mission in Gaul and the Tulle miracles (painting by Matteo Giovanetti 1344-1345)

A group of warriors and others in the embrasure of a window.

Two scenes from the ceiling of St.Martial. detail at right ▶

The Pope's bedroom, and the Chambre de Parement

Eastern wing of the private apartments. The Chambre de Parement

From the Grand Tinel, one enters the Pontiff's antichamber or dressing room, the **chambre du Parement,** (not yet restored), then the Pope's bedroom, the walls of which are ornamented with paintings depicting large foliated scrolls on which move birds and squirrels.

We leave the Benedict Palace by a short corridor, and enter that of Clement VI by the **Tour de la Garde-Robe** (1343).

The Pope's bedroom decorated with murals

Detail from mural and of tiling, Pope's bedroom

La Chambre du Cerf – hunting with hawks

Fishing from a pond

The beater

Hunting scene

The Northern Sacristy

At left, cast of the tomb of Philippe d'Alençon, vicar-general to Urban VI (the original is at Rome), in the Church of St.Marie du Transtevere ; At right, cast of a statue of the Emperor Charles IV who lived in the Palais des Papes in 1364.

The great chapel of Clement VI

By the **northern Sacristy** entrance is made to the **Grande Chapelle,** an immense nave 52 metres long, of sober lines, with traces of meridional Gothic. Against the eastern apse, the partly restored altar is the one on which the Popes used to celebrate services from the time of Innocent VI onwards. The **southern Sacristy,** or Revestiaire, shelters the facsimile of tombs of a number of the Avignon Popes.

**The
Southern
Sacristy
or 'revestiaire'**

Leaving the nave by the **loggia,** and the very mutilated doorway of the chapel, one may also see the large bay-window from which the Pope gave his benediction to the crowd assembled in the great Courtyard below.

Porch of the Grand Chapelle of Clement VI, much damaged in the XIX c., it still has large parts of its archivolt.

The window of 'Indulgences', overlooking the courtyard of honour. The mullions and fillings are a restitution much in controversy in the XX c.

By a magnificent two-flight stairway it is possible to climb to the **Grande Audience,** a fine hall wherein the ogival vaults rest on median pillars. This was the hall of justice where the **tribunal de la Rote** sat. In the eastern part of the room, a section of the vault is ornamented with fine frescoes depicting the Prophets, the last work in the palace carried out by Matteo Giovannetti (1352-1353).

Hall of the 'Grand Audience'

View of the north-west of Avignon (beginning of XVII c.). Drawing by Etienne Martelange in the Bibliothèque Nationale.

AVIGNON IN THE DAYS OF THE PAPACY

From the time of the coming of the papacy to Avignon, the population of the town increased suddenly in surprising proportions. It is true that the pontifical court was, at that time, the biggest in the world, and that its power of attraction was considerable.

In addition to the cardinals who, in the manner of the Pope, each kept up a small court, a crowd of business people of all sorts of nationalities gravitated to the Holy Father, forming what were called the "curiaux" or the "courtesans". This influx of strangers provoked a real shortage of lodgings, which was difficult to solve since the houses were small, and landlords demanded exorbitant sums in rent. It was thus found necessary to requisition rooms through the use of quartermasters who "assigned" lodgings to newcomers. It was thus that, under John XXII, 51 houses were appropriated, that is to say "livrée" to a single cardinal: the name remained in use to designate such quarters.

The extension of the town on the outside of the old Roman wall, already begun in the XIII c., was encouraged by the Popes who declared houses outside the walls to be free of taxes and from requisition, which brought about the rapid multiplication of 'bourgs' or 'bourguets'.

Within the walls, the city underwent rapid change. From Romanesque, it became Gothic little by little. A number of churches were rebuilt or embellished with subsidies from the cardinals, whilst the noble families or rich bourgeois built splendid homes.

In the second half of the XIV century, and from 1355, in view of the dangers from the **Grandes Compagnies,** attracted by the riches of the papacy, construction was begun of a new surrounding wall which would enclose the new 'bourgs', as well as numerous pleasure gardens. This wall was only completed under Urban V, and had a perimeter of more than 4,000 metres and enclosed in 1376, a population of about 30,000 inhabitants.

Since the XIII century, some of the principal ways through the town had been paved with stones taken from old beds of the River Rhône. This surface bore the name 'calade', a term still in use today. Generally speaking, the streets were narrow, twisting, and filled with pools, mud and foul smelling cess. Despite the watchfulness of the 'street masters', shop-stalls invaded the roadway, making passage difficult, the more so due to the semi-obscurity reigning because of the overhanging houses, whose roofs almost touched across the way.

Despite these multiple inconveniences, there was plenty of movement. Jugglers and acrobats attracted the gullible to all sorts of curiosities; for example a woman was exhibited in the Rue Grande-Fusterie who had no arms, but who carried out a number of domestic tasks with her feet.

From time to time these streets were the scene of magnificent processions and cavalcades, on the occasion of great pontifical ceremonies, coronation processions, or the solemn reception of a sovereign, such as the German Emperor Charles IV, or yet again the processions or "chevauchées" of the Pope, particularly liked by the Avignonnais. The streets were then swept, hung with draperies along the entire route, and illuminated at night. In 1389, for the visit of the King of France, Charles VI, the Avignon Bridge was illuminated with hundreds of candles.

But nothing equalled in magnificence the feasting which ended the celebrations at the crowning of the Pope. That of Clement VI took place on 19th May, 1342 in the vast Dominican convent, for at that time the Palais des Papes was not as big as it is now. The kitchen accounts give us the quantities of victuals bought for this gargantuan banquet: 118 fat cattle, 1 023 sheep, 101 calves, 914 kids, 60 pigs, 69 quintals of lard, 15 sturgeons, 300 pike, 10 471 hens, 1 446 ducks, 46 856 fresh cheeses, 39 980 eggs, 36 100 apples, 50 000 tarts. There were 26 000 plates, 2 200 bottles, 5 500 pitchers, etc. The kitchens and hearths burnt up 6 240 quintals of oak, whilst more than 100 quintals of wax were used for the making of torches and flambeaux. The number of guests has been estimated at over 3 000 for this grandiose feast, the total cost of which amounted to 14,132 florins, a considerable sum if you consider that six years later the same Pope bought the entire city of Avignon from Queen Jeanne for the price of 80 000 florins !

After visiting the Palais, different routes may be taken to see the town (see plan p.64). A small train-ride may also help. The following chapters deal with the principal centres of interest.

The square on a summer's day ▶

Cathedral of Notre-Dame des Doms. View of the nave and apse. The nave dates from mid XII century. The apse was rebuilt in 1672 and the baroque tribune is equally XVII century.

According to the most recent research, this fine building was built in three stages, during the course of the XII century; construction of the nave and narthex (beginning of the XII c.); addition of the cupola with lantern turret on the modified last span (about 1130-1140) and finally the building of a porch on the western face (second half of the XII c.). The apse which finished the Romanesque building was entirely destroyed in 1672 and replaced by a much bigger sanctuary. About the same time the baroque gallery was built along the lateral walls, a move which ended by disfiguring the old Romanesque nave, the first plan of which had already been spoiled by the addition of lateral chapels in a number of archways of the nave in gothic times;

The square bell-tower, destroyed in 1405 and rebuilt shortly afterwards in Romanesque tradition, was surmounted in 1859 by a gigantic statue of the Virgin in gilded lead.

The cupola which covers the last span is remarkable for the curious cantilever system which allowed the architect to change from an oblong plan to a square then to an octogonal one.

N.D. des Doms
Chapel of the Holy Sacrament

Paintings by Eugene Deveria
(1838-1851)

hoir of the Cathedral

ishop's Throne with baroque organ above

N.D. des Doms

The St. Roch Chapel

THE ROCHER DES DOMS

View from the Île de Barthelasse, showing the Pont St.Bénézet and the Rocher des Doms

The Rocher des Doms is an isolated block of cretaceous limestone which dominates the Rhône and the town by more than thirty metres. Recent discoveries have confirmed man's occupation in the most remote préhistoric periods. The early site was apparently at the foot of the promontory, then, in the course of centuries, the town slowly spread, to finally make up the town as we know it today. One may imagine the interest this rock caused, high above the river, and it is quite natural that first of all the cathedral and then the Palais des Papes were built on its slopes, as much for the beauty of the site as for the security it might offer. Today the plateau of the Doms is nicely laid out as a public garden offering visitors the charm of its pools and shades. It serves as a liaison between the Palais des Papes and the Pont St.Bénézet; it offers in addition a grandiose panorama over the Rhône, the town of Avignon, the Comtadine plain, the Mt.Ventoux and the Alpilles.

From the Rocher des Doms one may also reach the ramparts and visit the St.Nicholas Chapel on the Pont St.Bénézet.

The Doms' Garden

The Swan Lake

From the Garden towards the Palace Square

PONT SAINT BÉNÉZET

The Pont St.Bénézet and the Palais des Papes, from Ile Barthelasse

Built according to popular tradition by the shepherd Bénézet, the bridge was completed in January 1185, and dismantled on the orders of Cardinal St.Ange the day after the siege of 1226. Rebuilt between 1234 and 1237 at a higher level above the water, the construction then had twenty-two arches and was about 900 metres long. What remains of this today ? Very little, in fact. From the beginning, the bridge was a continuous worksite; in fact, undermined by the violent river currents, the arches frequently collapsed. They then had to be rebuilt or be replaced by wooden gangways. This continual fight against the river ended about 1660, at a time when the damage being too much, the people of Avignon renounced the continual repair.

The four arches which now remain date from work done about 1345-48 under the pontificate of Clement VI. They were heavily restored in the second half of the nineteenth century. The most ancient part of the construction is now the lower chapel, built on the second pile, and dedicated to St.Nicholas. Built on a semi-circular plan, the apse is vaulted in semi-dome and decorated with arcatures falling on to six small cylindrical or polygonal columns with corinthian capitals. The building of this part of the whole is very homogenous and must date to the twelfth century, on the contrary the nave, supported by diagonal ribs, is evidently later. The upper oratory is an heterogenerous addition, its apse being built in 1513, and its belfry still more recently.

The River Rhône and the Pont St.Bénézet

The Pont St.Bénézet linked the "Empire" with the "Kingdom", stepping over the Île de Barthelasse. The Avignonnais had the habit to go and dance on the island, under the arches of the bridge, from whence comes the popular song "Sous le Pont d'Avignon, on y danse, on y danse tous en rond".

The Petit Palais, north of the Place du Palais

This was, in the beginning, the livery of Cardinal Arnaud de Via († 1335), a nephew of Pope John XXII. The building next became the palace of the bishop of Avignon. It was partly rebuilt during the XV c. by Cardinal Alain de Coëtivy and by his successor Julien de la Rovère, who was to be the future Pope Julius II. It is to this period that the crenellated frontage dates, with its mullioned windows. At present the Petit Palais houses a museum of mediaeval art, which shows to the public a unique collection of primitive paintings dating from the XIII and XVI c., as well as numerous mediaeval sculptures of local provenance, a library and a study centre of mediaeval painting.

On the Place du Palais des Papes, we see also the front of the former Hôtel des Monnaies, or Mint, which has a very Italian aspect. The building is now occupied by the Avignon school of Music.

Some examples of the rich collection of paintings in the museum. Amongst the painters of the Italian School shown: Giotto, Perugina, Raphael.

The Place du Palais seen from N.D. des Doms

THE OLD MINT (Place du Palais)

This building was constructed in 1619 by the Papal vice-legate J.F. Bagni, during the legation of Cardinal Borghese. With its lower frontage of rebated ashlars, plus bands bearing large High-reliefs, out of scale, this curious facade is without question the most Italian in Avignon. The names of the master builder and artists who worked on this edifice are not known, but it is generally thought, in the absence of proof, that the Florentine sculptor Simone Bartolacci, who lived in Avignon from 1615 to 1634, was the author of the reliefs. The dragons and eagles which decorate it are part of the armorial bearings of the Pope Paul V and of Cardinal Borghese, his nephew.

Facade of the Hôtel des Monnaies (The Mint)

A view of the Avignon ramparts, built between 1355 and 1370, under the pontificates of Innocent VI and Urban V. This section, recently restored, has been cleared down to the level of the ancient ditch which fronted the walls.

The southern exit from the old town by the Cours Jean-Jaurès and the Porte de la République. This gateway did not exist in the Middle Ages, but was built in the XIX century by the architect Viollet-le-Duc.

View of the ramparts and the Palais in the setting sun

The Ramparts

Built between 1355 and about 1370, under the pontificates of Innocent VI and Urban V, the Avignon ramparts are among the best preserved in France. They are also among the longest, stretching almost four kilometres. In the beginning they were pierced by twelve gates, later by only seven. Today four of these gates are still standing : St.Lazare, St.Michel, St.Roch and La Ligne, the latter having been reconstructed in 1755 in classic style.

Topped with merlons and provided with machicolation, this long wall was defended by a succession of round towers and more numerous square ones, all open towards the interior. In fact, the walls of Avignon were only a first line of defence, in front of the formidable fortress of the Palais des Papes. Because of this, the walls were never a first class defence from a military point of view. The ditches were filled during the last century and certain parts of the walls were heavily restored by Viollet le Duc after 1860.

The walls of Avignon were built from soft limestone, also known under the name "pierre du midi", which is abundant throughout the region. "Time has given to these so perfect, so well jointed, so beautifully polished stones a uniform colour of dried leaves, which further enhances their beauty," wrote Stendhal.

A gate in the western ramparts

The first aerial view of Avignon, made from the basket of a balloon, about 1880. (Lithograph by Müller after a drawing by De Guesdon – Musée du Palais des Papes)

IN RECENT TIMES

The XVIII century ended with the thunderbolt of the Revolution and the fall of the French monarchy. Reunited with France on the 14th September, 1791, Avignon did not escape its share of the tumult. The war against the Comtat, reamining faithful to the Pope, the "massacre of La Glacière" on 16th and 17th October, 1791, which was, according to Michelet, "the hideous original of the September massacres", the federalist occupation, and the Terror were the principal episodes which illustrated this period of bloody troubles;

After the fall of Napoleon I and the reprisals of the "White Terror", (the assassination of Marshal Brune on 2nd August, 1815), Avignon restricted itself to the minor role of capital of an esentially agricultural **departement.** Only the violent electoral battles, the opening of the Cours Bonaparte (now the Cours Jean-Jaurès and Rue de la République), and the arrival of the railway troubled the otherwise monotonous rhythm of everyday life, though the part Avignon played in the rise of the Felibrige movement should not be forgotten.

The two most representative monuments erected in the XIX c. are the Town Hall and the Municipal Theatre in the Place de l'Horloge.

The first half of the XX c. was marked by the two World Wars, during the second of which Avignon suffered eighteen heavy bombing raids between May and August 1944.

The economic resurgence after the war allowed Avignon to become a regional metropolis, with activity principally directed towards commerce and tourism. Its picturesque site, numerous monuments from the past, annual International Festival of Dramatic Art in July and August, theatre, schools of music and art, and its museums have made Avignon a cultural centre of universal renown.

The Town Hall square about 1860 (litho: Musée Calvet)

The heart of Avignon, Place de l'Horloge

Front of the Town Hall, constructed between 1845 and 1851 by architects Jeoffroy and Feuchères

Place de l'Horloge. The Municipal Theatre, erected 1846-47 by architects Charpentier and Feuchères. certainly the best known building of those constructed in the XIX century.

THE TOWN HALL BELFRY
(Place de l'Horloge)

This is the last trace of the 'livrée d'Albano', or official residence in fact constructed by Cardinal Pierre Colonna († 1326). The high square tower with machicoulis was added to, in 1471, by a vaulted campanile surmounted by a spire and pinnacles, intended to house a clock and figures to mark the hours. The old Gothic 'livrée' was demolished in 1844-45 to allow the construction of the present Town Hall.

The Place de l'Horloge on a summer's day

Sun-drenched terraces, and daily musical performances in the shade of the plane trees.

The Baroncelli Mansion or Palais du Roure
(Place Louis-Le-Cardonnel – Rue du Collège du Roure)

This building was constructed at the end of the XV century for Pierre Baroncelli († 1498) a money-changer of Florentine origin. "The Baroncelli house, the most beautiful Gothic house in Avignon, is remarkable on the outside for its great door surmounted by a very singular design of entwined branches, seeming to come out of the wall itself, and with hardly any leaves. They surround a very worn shield topped by a large helmet supported by two standing figures now almost completely destroyed" (J. Girard). The building was very largely rebuilt at the end of the XVII century, especially inside, but the frontage has kept its Gothic style, with its two storeys of mullioned windows and flamboyant gateway.

The property of the City of Avignon, the Palais du Roure now houses the Institute of Mediterranean Studies, a rich literary, regional, historic and archaeologic library, as well as various collections.

The statue of F. Mistral on the Place Louis de Cardonnel

Palais du Roure

The doorway surmounted by sculptured entwined branches, and view of the inner court from the entrance porch.

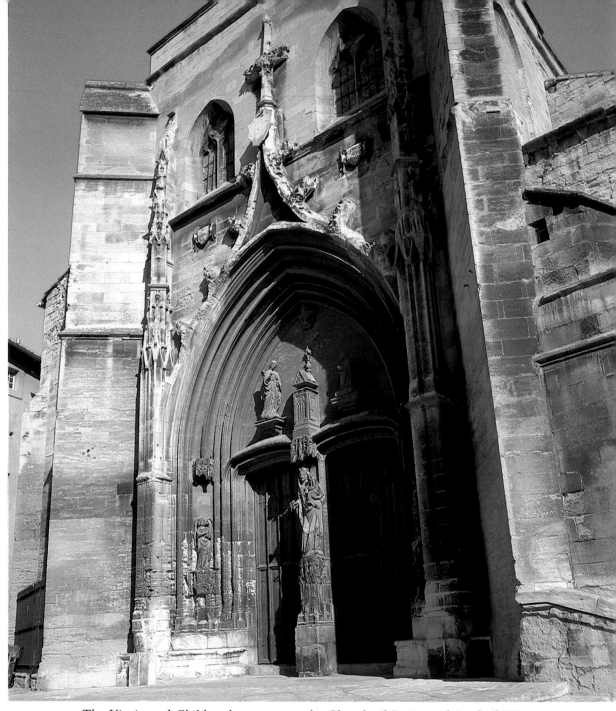

The Virgin and Child and entrance to the Church of St.Agricol (end of XV c.)

Built between 1321 and 1326 on the site of an older church, the parish church of St.Agricol was enlarged from the XV century by the addition of numerous lateral chapels. It was also at the end of the XV c. that the nave was lengthened by one span and the present facade added. The tympan was by Ferrier Bernard (1489), and represents the Annunciation, the Holy Spirit and God the Father. A fine Virgin and Child adorns the central pillar. The Belfry, in form of a square, was only added in 1740. The nave is lighted by high windows and ends with a pentagonal apse. There is no transept.

In the interior: paintings by Guillaume Grève, Pierre Parrocel, Nicolas Mignard, Sauvant, etc.; the main altar by Jean-Baptiste Péru (1767); at the end of the side-nave is the roodscreen of the Donis, a remarkable piece from the Renaissance, sculpted by Imbert Boachon (1525). See also, in the Brantes chapel, the sculptures by Jean Péru, (1650-1723), and a Virgin and Child by Coysevox. Near the entrance is a very fine stoup in white marble from the XVI century.

A look at the exterior of the apse (Rue Félicien-David) will show that it was built on Gallo-Roman ruins.

The Place Crillon recently renovated with, at right, the old Comédie

The old Comedy Theatre
(Place Crillon)

Built between 1732 and 1734 by Thomas Lainée, the old comedy, facing the Porte de l'Oulle, shows an elegant front with Ionic pilasters crowned with a triangular pediment decorated with a rayonnant head of Apollo. The edifice is surmounted by a balustrade bearing four stone vases. The former theatre closed its doors in 1824 and was sold to private interests who destroyed the interior, whilst the fine front was spoiled by the placing of windows and the turning of the ground floor into commercial premises. Very fortunately the building has recently been acquired by the City and restored under the direction of the Historic Monument Service.

View of the front of the old Comédie, built by Thomas Lainée (1732-34)

THE CALVET MUSEUM

The interior court of the Hôtel, now entrance to the Museum

The de Villeneuve-Martignan mansion
(65, Rue Joseph-Vernet)

Built between 1742 and 1753 by Jean-Baptiste and François Franque, for Joseph-Ignace de Villeneuve, this magnificent mansion is probably the most sumptuous house in Avignon. "Its buildings, with facades crowned with balustrades, are grouped around an entrance court and garden" (J. Girard). The sculptures are by Pierre Bondon. A suite of five salons ornamented with woodwork has been preserved north of the garden. Presently, the Hôtel de Villeneuve houses the collections of the Calvet Museum.

See the magnificent salons where hang numerous paintings of the French, Italian, Flemish, Dutch Schools, etc., also the fine wrought-iron collection of N. Biret. At the bottom of the garden, the new acquisitions and a gallery of Vauclusian prehistory.

Furniture and fireplace (XVII c.) in the museum

Louis Le Nain:
Portrait
of a nun (1644)

German school (XVI c.),
Jesus Christ
going to Calvary

Portrait of a woman
attributed to J.F. Voet
(1639-1700)

Pierre Mignard:
Madame de Montespan
and her son,
the Duc du Maine

Hall of Wrought Ironwork
(Collection Noël Biret)

Church of the monastery-college of St.Martial, (XIV-XV c.), seen from the Square Agricol Perdiguier

The church, construction of which began in 1383, was in the beginning part of a benedictine monastery. The nave has been almost entirely destroyed, but a fine pentagonal apse remains, of elegant line, at present used by the Evanlegical Reformed Church. The steeple, built in the XV century, is of the Avignon type of the period, with characteristic crocketted spire mounted on a square tower with octogonal drum.

THE CHURCH OF ST.MARTIAL

In the square, vestiges of the cloister of the old monastery

THE MUSÉE LAPIDAIRE
(Rue de la République)

This museum is the custodian of precious vestiges of the past history of Avignon. Since the prehistoric period, every era has left the mark of its passage in stone. Other than discoveries concerning Avignon itself, such as the remains of a Gallo-Roman arch, the museum has numerous other pieces discovered in the region such as the Tarasque from Noves, the Warrior from Vachères, the Lion from Mornas, etc.

Facade of the chapel of the Jesuit college (1661), Rue de la République, now the Musée Lapidaire;

Statuary and votive stelae in the Musée Lapidaire

Towing on the river Durance (found at Cabrières d'Avignon)

THE CHURCH OF ST.PIERRE

(Facade, Place St.Pierre, apse and lateral entrance Place Bir-Akeim)

The front of the Church of St.Pierre
An exuberance of flamboyant Gothic

Of very ancient origin, this church was rebuilt starting in 1358, continuing until 1525. Its style is Meridional Gothic, and is notable for its exuberant facade (1512) where the flamboyant style begins to be mixed with the first signs of the Renaissance. This facade is ornamented with an elegant statue of the Virgin and Child attributed to Jean Péru (early XVIII c.); its decoration is completed by two doors in solid walnut, the leaves of which, sculpted by Antoine Volard in 1551, show St.Jerome, St.Michael and the Annunciation. The Belfry (late XV c.) is certainly the finest in Avignon. The building was modified in 1854 by the addition of a second nave.

The original statue of the central pillar has been replaced by an elegant Virgin and Child attributed to the local painter and sculptor Jean Péru (early XVIII c.)

The magnificent portals in solid walnut at the entrance, carved by Antoine Volard in 1551, representing St.Jerome, St.Michael and the Annunciation

The Annunciation portal ▶

Interior and chevet of the St.Pierre Church

The chevet and elegant belfry (late XV c.) with its hooked spire, which is one of the most typical of Avignon Gothic style.

The interior is in very simple style, but the choir is decorated with XVII c. gilded woodwork, to a design by La Valfenière, a sumptuous group comprising fourteen paintings and twenty four small painted panels.

In the Chapel of the Souls in Purgatory is a famous Renaissance retable sculpted by Imbert Baochon (1526) for Perrinet Parpaille. between the second and third chapels, a superb throne from the XV c. in white sculpted stone, from which the original statuettes have been lost. See also various pictures by Guillaume Grève, Simon de Châlons, Nicolas Mignard, and Pierre Parrocel. The eastern end of the second nave is closed by a Descent to the Tomb, in stone, from the XVI century.

A view of the choir, decorated with a sumptuous amount of gilded woodwork from the XVII century, to the designs of De la Valfenière.

View from the choir of the nave; at right the XV century throne; in background, the organ loft.

THE CHURCH OF SAINT DIDIER

(Entrance now from place St.Didier)

This is certainly one of the most characteristic monuments in Provençal Gothic. It was completed in three years, from 1356 to 1359, and shows a remarkable homogeneity. It comprises a nave with six spans, completed by a pentagonal apse and bordered with chapels established between the powerful butresses.

In the Baptismal Fonts chapel are large frescoes (**Déposition de Croix** and **Vierge de l'Annonciation**), the work of a Florentine studio about 1360.

The choir contains a very fine main altar in sculpted marble by J.B. Péru (1750) as well as the remains of the monumental tomb of Cardinal de Déaux († 1355), who founded the church.

In the Chapel of Notre-Dame de Compassion, the first on the right in the nave, see the famous marble altar-piece by Francesco Laurana, **Le Portement de la Croix** or **Notre Dame du Spasme,** one of the oldest works of the French Renaissance (1478), which once graced the Church of the Celestins.

Facade of the Chapel of the Black Penitents (XVIII c.)

Rue Carreterie, with the belfry of the Grands Augustins

The Chapel of the Black Penitents of Mercy, built and richly ornemented in the XVII c., underwent a number of transformations from 1739 to 1755: Addition of an anti-chapel and construction of the facade to plans of Thomas Lainée, succeeded by J.B. Franque. This remarkable frontage is decorated with an immense 'burst of glory' or aureola in bas-relief with two angels who carry the emblem of the brotherhood – the head of St.John the Baptist on a platter.

The 'Grands Augustins'

This convent, founded in 1261, was situated near and to the south of that of the 'Grand Carmes'. The convent church, reconstructed in the XIV c., was entirely destroyed in the Revolution. There only remains the picturesque tower, strangely rising above the Rue Carrèterie. Built from 1372-77 on the same plan as that of the Carmelites, it was shortened about 1562 and finished by an iron campanile. A public clock was placed on the tower from 1497.

Other noteworthy buildings in Avignon

Hôtel de Crillon (7, Rue Roi-René)

Built 1648-49 for Louis III de Berton, Baron de Crillon, grand-child of Crillon le Brave. The architect was Domenico Borboni, from Bologna, which explains the typical Italian style. The facade is ornamented with much decoration consisting of medaillions, symbols, masks, cornucopias, garlands, etc. These are tentatively attributed to

Jean-André Borde. The buildings are grouped around a court-of-honour communicating, by a portico, with the entrance vestibule where one can see the majestic double stairs with stone balustrade, ornamented with huge copper balls.

Hôtel Fortia de Montréal (8 & 10 Rue du Roi-René)

Facing the Hôtel de Crillon, the Hôtel de Montréal is decorated more soberly. Built from 1637, to designs by François de Royers de la Valfernière at the expense of Paul de Forta de Montréal, Captain of the Royal French Navy in the Port of Marseilles.

Hôtel de Caumont (5, Rue Violette and Boulevard Raspail)

This fine construction was put up between 1720 and 1751 by Jean-Baptiste and François Franque for Joseph de Seytres, Marquis de Caumont, scholar and writer, who died in 1745 before the work was finished. The same year, the famous Duc d'Ormont died here, a great English aristocrat and Jacobite who took refuge at Avignon with the Pretender James Stuart. "The Hôtel de Caumont is one of the most perfect constructions by the Franques, one of those where they have best found the right dimensions, the just proportions and the elegance of the outline" (J. Girard). Recently restored, the Hôtel de Caumont now houses the Faculty of Letters of Avignon.

Hôtel de Galéans-Gadagne (7, Rue Violette and Boulevard Raspail)

Next to the Hôtel de Caumont, this was built from 1751, also to plans by Franque, for the Duc de Galéans de Gadagne. It is more modest than its neighbour, has also recently been restored, and is used by the same Faculty. The two houses thus form an interesting ensemble.

Church of St.Symphorien or the 'Grand carmes' (Entrance, Place des Carmes)

The parish church of Saint Symphorien is in reality the former church of the old Great Carmelite convent, built in the early years of the XIV c. in Meridional Gothic style on the site of a XIII c. edifice. Its facade dates to the XV century, the nave, first roofed in wood, received its present vault in 1836. The body of the church, the biggest in Avignon is flanked by fourteen lateral chapels. The chapel dedicated to N.D. du Mont Carmel contains a statue of the Virgin of gilded wood, attributed to Burnus (XVIII c.). In the Chapel of the Crucifix there is a fine altar of gilded wood and, above, a superb Calvary of painted wood comprising Christ, the Virgin and St.John (early XVI c.). See also the pictures by Guillaume Grève, Nicolas Mignard, Pierre Parrocel, Auguste Bigand, etc., and the stone baptismal fonts from the XVI century.

The belfry is composed of a square tower with hooked spire on an octogonal drum pierced by narrow lights (XIV c.).

North of the church, the fine ogival vaulted cloister has recently been cleared and restored; it is used for theatre productions during the annual Festival of Dramatic Art.

Other Churches and Belfries

The Church of the Celestins (Rue Saint-Michel and Place des Corps-Saints)

Built in several stages between 1396 and 1424 on the site of the tiny cemetery of St.Michel or paupers cemetery. The architect Perrin Morel constructed the apse, transept and the two spans of the choir between 1396 and 1406. Twenty years later, a new span was added, but the church, designed on a vast scale, was never finished. To the south is a fine Gothic cloister which is now used as stage during the drama Festival.

The Church of the Cordeliers or Grey Friars.

Only a few traces beside a truncated tower remain at the beginning of Rue des Teinturiers. The famous Laure, who inspired the poet Petrarch, is said to have been buried here.

Chapel of La Visitation (Rue Paul-Saïn and Place Pignotte)

This chapel, now dedicated to the Holy Sacrament, is a typical example of Jesuit style. Founded by Cardinal Philonardi, Archbishop of Avignon, it was constructed by François de la Valfenière between 1631 and 1638. The interior is richly sculpted, by Jean-André Borde. Above the transept rises a dome of good proportions.

The St.Jean-le-Vieux Tower (Place Pie)

This crenellated tower is the last vestige of the commandery of the Order of St.John of Jerusalem, a vast group of buildings dating back to the XIII c. and which were destroyed in 1893 to widen the square. The tower was raised in the XIV century, badly restored in the XIX c. and fitted with a clock.

One of the last houses with corbelling in old Avignon.

THE MUSEUMS

*Other than the museums
already mentioned;
Musée du Petit Palais (page 38)
Musée Lapidaire (page 53)
Musée Calvet (page 50)
other establishments
offer much of interest.*

The entrance to Petit Palais

Requien Museum (67, Rue Joseph-Vernet)

The Musée Requien, or Natural History Museum, set up in the former Hôtel de Raphélis de Soissans (XVIII c.) is principally a centre for research and study. It has the fifth largest herbarium in France (about 250 000 specimens) accessible to specialists, laboratories and a large reference library. On the ground floor, six public rooms hold a permanent exhibition on the geology, flora and fauna of Vaucluse (entrance free).

Vouland Museum (17, Rue Victor-Hugo)

This museum has a collection of furniture (XVII-XVIII c.), ceramics (Moustiers, Montpellier, Marseilles), as well as various precious items (entrance free).

Maison Jean Vilar (Rue de Mons)

In the old Hôtel de Crochans (XVIII c.) are assembled many memories of great actors, the **Théâtre National Populaire,** the festival of Avignon, etc., also a large library and videotheque dealing with arts of the theatre. Frequent exhibitions.

In the renovated centre of town, a pedestrian street...
In the town, the fountain in the Place de Corps Saints (Second empire)

Villeneuve, an aerial view: in the foreground, the Tour de Philippe le Bel, in middle distance, the Fort St.André

VILLENEUVE-LÈS-AVIGNON

Villeneuve-lès-Avignon is situated on the right bank of the Rhône, facing the city of the Popes. Its origin goes back to Mount Andaon where, from the V century, there was a hermitage where Saint Casarie lived and died. In the X century a Benedictine monastery was founded on the spot, and rapidly grew in importance. This was the famous Abbey of St.André, around which grew a small settlement, mostly composed of quarrymen and stone-workers.

At first placed under the tenure of Avignon, after the capitulation of the city in 1226 the abbey concluded a treaty with King Louis VIII: this was renewed in 1292 by Philippe le Bel who granted a charter of freedom to the inhabitants, which resulted in the extension of the settlement which then became a "new town" (**ville neuve**). The King also built the tower which carries his name at the head of the Pont St.Bénézet;

The installation of the Papacy at Avignon in the XIV c. only increased this growth. The new town filled with rich residences and cardinals' palaces, whilst its defences were reinforced by Jean le Bon who built a long line of defensive walling on the summit of the plateau.

After the departure of the Popes, Villeneuve went through a less brilliant period. only the XVII and XVIII centuries brought again a certain richness in monuments and art, mostly due to the Carthusians and to the monks of St.André who enlarged and embellished their buildings.

The principal monuments and curiosities in Villeneuve are Philippe le Bel's Tower, the Collegiate Church of Notre-Dame, the museum, the Monastery La Chartreuse du Val des Bénédictions, and the Fort st.André.

The Tower of Philip the Fair

This is the sole remaining part still standing of what was a large defensive group at the end of the bridge leading to Avignon, on the Kingdom side. The tower was at first just a ground floor and first floor covered with flagstones, but a second floor was added in the XIV century. It is possible to climb to these three levels and to reach the top platform where the sentinel stood. In the Middle Ages, a number of 'livrées' belonging to the Cardinals stood near the tower. We may mention that of Cardinal Napoleon Orsini († 1342), and Bertrand de Déaux († 1355), the latter house also being known as the "Hôtel des Monnaies".

The Fort St.André

Villeneuve developed considerably between the building of the Tower (1293-1307) and that of the Fort St.André (about 1362-1368). By building the latter, Jean le Bon wished to emphasise, it seems, the power of the King's town in the face of Avignon, proud and arrogant Imperial city become a "second Rome". Note also that this period at the end of the Middle Ages was that of terror from the "Grandes Compagnies", when the new Avignon ramparts were also built.

The crenellated walls of the Fort St.André enclose the summit of Mount Andaon, twin and rival to the Rocher des Doms, also inhabited since prehistoric times. This powerful curtain-wall is dominated and commanded by high round towers: La Roquette to the north, La Tour Brûlée to the east, la Tour des Masques (or Les Sorcières) to the south-west, and to the south, facing Avignon, twin towers. The latter, semi-cylindrical, topped with a crenellated crown with machi colation, framed and defended the only entrance to the fort, constituting with the small castle between them a formidable piece of military architecture, worthy of Carcassone. "The whole of these fortifications is certainly the strongest, the best built and most perfected of all the region," (J. Girard).

Inside the walls of the fort, the limestone plateau is covered by ruins of habitations, remains of a hamlet now disappeared from which is left a tiny and charming Romanesque chapel: Notre-Dame de Belvezet (late XII c.). The Benedictine Abbey of St.André, which occupied the top of Mt.Andaon, had been built at the beginning of the XII century and its church was consecrated in 1118 by Pope Gelasius II. For long rival to the powerful St.Ruf Abbey in Avignon, it was almost entirely reconstructed by the monks of St.Maur, to the point that the buildings which remain today date for the most part to the XVIII century.

At the foot of the Fort St.André, La Chartreuse du Val de Bénédiction

La Chartreuse, Monastery of the Carthusian Monks

In the main street, where one may still see large traces of the houses of the Cardinals (livrée de Montirac and especially de Thurroye), there is the main door of La Chartreuse, founded by Pope Innocent VI in 1356, at first dedicated to St.John the Baptist, then to the Val de Bénédic

The Collegiate church of Notre-Dame

Here construction is due to a nephew of Pope John XXII, the Cardinal Arnaud de Via, who founded a college of twelve canons, and who wished to be buried there. The building, consecrated in 1333, is in Meridional Gothic style and recalls by its simplicity the Church of St.Didier in Avignon. The three western spans have culs-de-lampe richly sculpted (scenes of the life of Christ). The belfry is a powerful square tower with crenellated platform. the building contains numerous works of art amongst which is the tomb of Arnaud de Via, by Jean Lavenier, fragments of the inscription of Saint Casarie (VI c.), the throne of the Abbots of St.André, in white marble (XVII c.), paintings by Philippe de Champagne, Nicolas Mignard, Reynaud Levieux, and a superb main-altar in variegated marble,

tion in 1362. The church was consecrated in 1358 by Cardinal de Boulogne in the presence of the Pope. Different members of the Pope's family, notably the Cardinals Ardouin and Etienne Aubert, and Selva de Montirac, enlarged the convent and loaded it with privileges which made this monastery one of the most opulent in the Order.

decorated with a recumbent Christ of very high class by Antoine Duparc († 1755). In the sacristy there is a Virgin in ivory of exceptional quality (XIV c.), the gift of Cardinal Arnaud de Via to the Collegial.

A cloister, fairly well preserved, with galleries having diagonal ribbed vaults, is to the north of the church.

The Museum

The old Hospice, which is to be found in the market street, lined with arcades, is the proud possessor of the "Couronnement de la Vierge" (1453-54) by Enguerrand Quarton, one of the major items of the Avignon School, and others by Simon de Châlons, Renaud le Vieux, Pierrre and Nicolas Mignard, etc.

THE OLD TOWN: THE PRINCIPAL SITES AND MONUMENTS OF AVIGNON

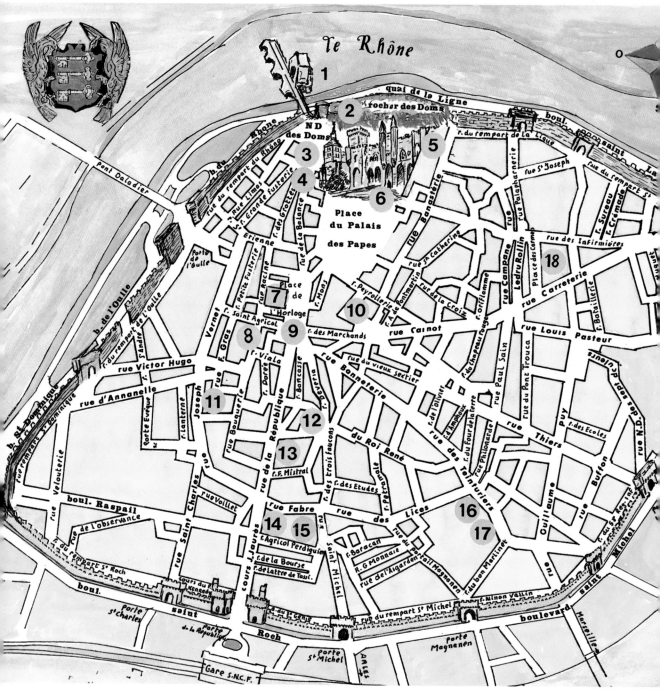

The monuments and museums of Avignon are situated in the interior of the walls, which follow the outlines of the old town, the ancient narrow quarters of which have been arranged as pedestrian precincts.

1. *Pont St.Bénézet, or the 'Pont d'Avignon'*
2. *N.D. des Doms, the Cathedral and garden of the Doms*
3. *The Petit Palais (Collection Campana)*
4. *Hôtel des Monnaies or Mint, (Conservatory of Music)*
5. *Black Penitents' Church*
6. *The Palais des Papes*
7. *Place de l'Horloge, Hôtel de Ville, Theatre and Belfry*
8. *St.Agricol Church*
9. *Hôtel de Baroncelli-Javon (palais du Roure)*
10. *Church of St.Pierre, Place Pie*
11. *Musée Calvet (paintings, furniture, ironwork).*
12. *Church of St.Didier (sculpture, frescoes, retable)*
13. *Musée Lapidaire, (Jesuit College)*
14. *Tourist Office: Information*
15. *Church of St.Martial, Square Agricol Perdiguier*
16. *Grey penitents' Chapel*
17. *Church of the Cordeliers, St.Joseph's College*
18. *Church of St.Symphorien*